Why Children Should Read

7 Secrets To Raising Intelligent Children In A Challenging World

Frank Dixon

Before we begin, I have something special waiting for you. An action-packed 1 page printout with a few quick & easy tips taken from this book that you can start using today to become a better parent right now!

It's my gift to you, free of cost. Think of it as my way of saying thank you to you for purchasing this book.

Claim your download of Profoundly Positive Parenting with Frank Dixon by scanning the QR code below and join my mailing list.

Sign up below to grab your free copy, print it out and hang it on the fridge!

Sign Up By Scanning The QR Code With Your Phone's Camera To Be Redirected To A Page To Enter Your Email And Receive INSTANT Access To Your Download

Before we jump in, I'd like to express my gratitude. I know this mustn't be the first book you came across and yet you still decided to give it a read. There are numerous courses and guides you could have picked instead that promise to make you an ideal and well-rounded parent while raising your children to be the best they can be.

But for some reason, mine stood out from the rest and this makes me the happiest person on the planet right now. If you stick with it, I promise this will be a worthwhile read.

In the pages that follow, you're going to learn the best parenting skills so that your child can grow to become the best version of themselves and in doing so experience a meaningful understanding of what it means to be an effective parent.

Notable Quotes About Parenting

"Children Must Be Taught How To Think, Not What To Think."

– Margaret Mead

"It's easier to build strong children than to fix broken men [or women]."

- Frederick Douglass

"Truly great friends are hard to find, difficult to leave, and impossible to forget."

– George Randolf

"Nothing in life is to be feared, it is only to be understood. Now is the time to understand more, so that we may fear less."

– Scientist Marie Curie

Table of Contents

Introduction

"The more that you read, the more things you will know. The more that you learn, the more places you'll go."

~Dr. Seuss

If you search for "how to increase intelligence" on Google, you will come across many ideas, from eating lots of turmeric to taking fish oil supplements daily. Some articles boast about how enrolling in a new language course is the way to do it, while others would stick with the old guns, promoting mind-stimulating activities like solving puzzles, doing crosswords, or learning a new musical instrument. Sure, they all help and promise an improvement, but why go through all of it when the answer is as simple as reading?

There is no better way to improve cognitive functioning than by reading. It is the best brain exercise there is and also the cheapest. Reading, whether fiction or nonfiction, has the power to relieve stress, build vocabulary, and improve comprehension and memory. Reading promises the same benefits as exercise provides to the body. It sharpens the brain and keeps it active and young.

Countless studies endorse the idea that reading is a great habit to develop among children. Books give children new worlds to think about. They spark creativity. They stimulate the imagination. They reveal to children the many secrets about the world, various cultures, and the people that practice them.

As parents and mentors, we are in an excellent position to ensure that reading books become a part of our child's daily routine. Diving into a good book opens gateways to new information and knowledge. This is an ideal way to build vocabulary and comprehension skills in children. Readers have been known to score better in general tests than non-readers.

Furthermore, early reading skills promise higher intelligence in adulthood. This was scientifically explored by researchers from the University of Edinburgh and King's College London (Ritchie et al., 2014). In the experiment, the results of reading and intelligence of 1890 pairs of identical twins, part of the Twins Early Development Study, were compared. These tests were taken by identical twins at the ages of seven, nine, ten, twelve, and sixteen.

The reason for using genetic twins was to eliminate any differences that might affect the results and findings. Since the twins were brought up in the same family environments, it allowed researchers to gain a better insight into their lives and learning abilities. There were, however, some limitations, like one of the twins receiving an inspiring friend that loved to read or a teacher that made them fall in love with the magic of reading.

After the comparisons were made, the researchers found that the twin with better early reading ability would go on to achieve better grades at school as well as do better in other intelligence tests too. This was a significant and astonishing conclusion, as it proved that reading did improve intelligence—both verbal and non-verbal.

But that's not all. Another study found that children aged eight to ten who loved to read or had the habit of reading from an early age had more white matter in their brain than those who didn't read or liked reading ("Carnegie Mellon scientists discover first evidence of brain rewiring in children," 2020). The increase in white matter in the brain improves system-wide communication. When communication between the brain and the body improves, information is processed at a quicker rate. Signal transmission increased efficiently, and the experiment revealed that the children could read better.

These studies prove that if there is an easy and promising way to develop intelligence, it is by developing the habit of reading among children. In this guide, we are going to further explore this and see how reading changes the brain, how to pick the right books for your children, when you should start reading to infants, and how parents can instill good reading habits in this time when technology seems to have taken over.

Hopefully, by reading this, you will be able to raise adults who love to read and make time for it despite their busy schedules. They will experience the joy that reading brings and learn how it enriches the soul and the mind with positivity and hope—something we can all use a little bit of.

Chapter 1:

Why Read?

Infants and children are like sponges. They soak up practically everything that they see around them. They learn through experiences. They learn from their parents and siblings and other children they play with. They pick up similar habits. From sleeping in the same posture to chewing like their father, some are genetically transferred. As for habits like reading, travel, and organization—they are the ones they pick from us.

When we read to babies and children, or with them, their mind is at work. Every word they hear and the lessons and messages are taken in. A story, whether it is about a young boy lost in the woods calling on his parents or about a young girl trying to find her place in a new world and culture, helps them visualize the struggles and sense the emotions others experience. They take in those lessons and meaningful messages to their heart. They emulate the same actions as their favorite character.

If their character has the habit of praying before bedtime, they start doing the same. If their favorite superhero wears a cape, they want one too. If their favorite protagonist is out fighting crime, they speak up for those who can't fend for themselves.

That is the power of a good book. It changes us for the better. It isn't always about how it expands one's knowledge; it is about how it makes us feel at the end of the day and what positive changes it brings to our thoughts.

Reading to your child, at any age, is as exciting as this. Moreover, it is beneficial for their brain development as well. In this chapter, we will look at some of the most important and pivotal advantages of why parents should instill good reading habits in young children.

Let's Talk Benefits

Speaking of the benefits, the first is improved literacy skills. No matter how basic or complex, a book improves your child's literacy skills. They may not grasp every word or message, but they can enjoy and experience how it feels to read. The joy that comes from hearing a good story will motivate them to read by themselves. This joy also allows them to fully embrace the message and analyze what's being said instead of simply turning pages from left to right.

Reading to infants, meanwhile, can help them with stimulating the part of the brain that processes language acquisition. Being exposed to new words and emotions also improves a child's vocabulary and emotional intelligence. They may come across an emotion or word that they haven't experienced, and it can be an enlightening event and serve as a great conversation starter. For example, your child may not be familiar with the word "rude" and question you about it. You can teach them what it means and how to respond when one invokes it.

Reading can guarantee some excellent bonding time between you and your child where you explore new worlds and words together. Reading is a great opportunity for you to connect. You can read to them in bed, go book shopping together, or get a library card so that you can borrow books for your child from the nearest public library. One study confirms that reading to your child every night makes them feel secure (Duursma et al., 2008).

With a book, you can make your child understand various concepts like climate change, political war, violence, media bias, and many such topics and why it's important to know about them. If your children are too young for this, you can begin with the simpler things like improving their general knowledge about the world. For example, you can get encyclopedias, a book about the flags of the world, a book that lists continents, countries, and capitals, etc. All this will help them when they start school.

As explained before, reading can help young children express themselves better using a wide range of words and emotions. This will come in handy when they start socially interacting with children their age and validate their emotions and feelings as well. When you read a story to your child, it consists of various characters, some of which are good and bad. Children have a natural inclination to admire the character doing good. This proves that they are empathetic by nature.

As they grow older, this empathy can take a back seat as they start to assess all things rationally. Empathy, in today's world, is a gift. People who are blessed with a kind heart and pure soul are the most cherished. Then, the cause and effect relationship in stories develops their analytical skills too. They become more curious about why someone does something and what consequences they have to pay. This makes them feel responsible for their actions and words.

When you read to your child, you allow them to immerse themselves in different worlds, meet new people, and learn about their culture and traditions. They can learn about some unique festivals celebrated around the globe and their significance. They can learn about the stories of people who changed the world for the better and become inspired. They can learn about the struggles and hardships of several tribes, groups, and ethnicities and develop a soft spot for them. A good book has the power to take them to a town, city, or country without actually traveling.

Hearing you read a story also involves listening. The more attentive they are, the more they will understand. Imagine reading to them every night. Their listening and comprehension skills will improve every time. According to experts, listening comes before reading. Meaning, if a child can listen, they can learn to read too (Wolf et al., 2018).

Reading also improves concentration and attentiveness (Castro, 2015). Children who can remain engaged in a story for long periods have a less difficult time sitting still in school and remain focused on the coursework. Improved concentration also means that they will encode new information better than others who are easily distracted.

Since reading is an immersive activity, it can lead to higher levels of creativity and imagination. When a child reads a book about a distinguished character, they can create a mental picture of them based on the description, personality, and traits. They can visualize the environment and settings and predict what's going to happen next.

All of this might seem like a normal thing, but just for a second, look at what's happening. It all begins in the mind, where the child starts to picture a character. Then, based on their actions and traits, they can predict the next step the character will take. If that isn't quick learning, then what is?

A book opens so many doors for creativity. The power of imagination can lead to greater creativity and help young minds use most of their brain to do things using out-of-the-box methodologies.

A child's critical thinking skills are also nurtured when parents read to them from an early age. Scientists believe that when children read, it activates several areas in their brain connected to visual imagery and language comprehension. These skills are highly valued when the children start kindergarten because they feel more ready to read (High, 2014).

Speaking of academic success, other studies suggest that the more words a child learns, the stronger their language skills will be. The more prepared they are to read, the better they will read. The same study goes on to reveal that readers are more likely to graduate from high school than non-readers. Students who are exposed to reading before school are more likely to do well in formal education settings (Allen & Kelly, 2015). Researchers at the University of Michigan highlighted these five essential reading skills for their healthy academic development.

1. Phonics: Knowing how to connect the letters of written words with their sound.
2. Phonemic Awareness: Knowing how to identify, ear, and play with different sounds in spoken language.
3. Reading Comprehension: Knowing how to understand the meaning of what's being read.
4. Vocabulary: Knowing a vast range of words to express themselves and communicate effectively.
5. Fluency: Knowing how to read the text quickly and accurately.

These skills, along with thinking and analytical skills, help children excel in their academics and have a broader perspective about life.

Books also offer children an opportunity to read about real-life situations in a way that's understandable and relatable. Children love reading books that feature characters of the same age. They get inspired by their lives, their will to do good, and actions that result in the welfare of others. Such stories model discipline and mannerism in children. It also prepares them to deal with something uncertain on their own because they think they have it in them to face it. Why? It is because their favorite character did so in the story. Therefore, it is ideal to read to children stories about the first day of school, moving houses, going to a dentist, or getting a flu shot, as it mentally prepares them for those circumstances.

Finally, they can also learn how to cope with situations that appear stressful or difficult, like a medical emergency at home. If a child knows that they need to call 911 right away, they can help the injured get medical assistance promptly. Similarly, if they are going through a particularly difficult time like the loss of a loved one or separation between parents, reading to them stories about similar cases can help them cope with the situation in a better, more composed manner.

Differences Between a Reader and a Non-Reader

A lot of parents debate that these are all skills that a child can pick up on their own as they start school. They can develop empathy by forming social ties, learning about different cultures through movies and coursework, discovering new places by traveling and going on vacations, and picking up critical thinking and problem-solving skills when they study for tests.

It may seem as simple as that, but the answer to this is actually rather complex. To put it simply, think of it as a world divided between readers and non-readers. The difference between these two mindsets is unbridgeable, and no other activity can replace the need for reading.

For example, readers are absorbers; non-readers aren't. Readers know how to use the knowledge they have been blessed with. They know what to make of it. They can dissect and comprehend it better thanks to their creativity and imagination. Non-readers are simply broadcasters. When provided with new knowledge, they don't know what to make of it. They simply pass it on without gaining anything new from it.

Readers know their stuff. Non-readers run on empty. Readers are fully committed to the art of reading: Whether it's a particular author or genre that they enjoy reading, they are into it a hundred percent. Non-readers, sadly, are unable to form such an intimate and important connection with any book. They will read it for the sake of reading and close it once they are done. If anything, they will miss out on the entire message that the book or the author is trying to give, masked in their words and writing style.

This enables readers to develop a curiosity about the world around them too. They can see and feel things that aren't there. They can pick up on non-verbal gestures and body language. They can sense what someone is going through by reading their face. They can offer more sensible advice, backed by valid justification and facts. Non-readers can't. They don't have that curiosity in them to know what's happening around them. They are self-absorbed. Readers, on the other hand, are obsessed with the world beyond them.

Readers are also happier than non-readers, according to a study by SuperSummary. It is an online resource that offers in-depth study guides for interested people. After conducting a survey, the resource confirmed that readers are more satisfied with their lives than people who don't identify themselves as readers ("Are readers more successful?" 2021).

Readers also have more white brain matter than non-readers. Researchers at Stanford University found that reading for pleasure increases blood flow for different regions of the brain, simultaneously exercising multiple complex cognitive functions (Phillips, 2012).

Readers can focus on the backstory. This is due to increased empathy and compassion for others. Readers don't just hear what others tell them; they also hear what they can't or don't. Unlike non-readers, readers don't make snap judgments. Since readers have been exposed to various worlds and people in books, read about their actions and what caused them, they understand that every action has a backstory and complicated context to it. This is also another reason why readers appear so patient and understanding. They can relate to you by being in your shoes.

Chapter 2:

Age-Appropriate Reading

Since reading to kids is both a pleasurable and promising activity, a lot of parents question when the right time to begin reading to kids is and, more importantly, what they should read. Infancy seems like an age too young. "All babies do is eat, sleep, and repeat." But this isn't the case. They hear too. They listen. They see things and remember your voice. They become fonder of you, your voice, your love, and your touch. They learn to become attentive. They learn how to pick up different tones of voice. They observe the many gestures you do with your hands, even though they don't understand most of them.

Then, as they begin to grow, their interactions with you become stronger and more devoted. Reading doesn't only remain a time to hear a new story; it becomes a time to bond and spend some quality time together. Their habits start to form. You notice them trying to imitate what you read by picking up a book and casually scrolling through the pages. You notice that they begin to identify different characters like a cat or dog. All these things happen because you decided to read. Your children develop a passion for reading because you read to them from the start. They love books because one of their earliest memories involves you holding one in your hands.

Then again, what to read, how to pick the right books, and determining if your child can understand what is being read to them and remember are questions that come to mind. In this chapter, let us take that worry off your shoulders and present you with a step-by-step, age-appropriate guide to commence reading to your young ones with confidence.

Age-Appropriate Reading Manual for Parents

The birth of a child is one of the most precious moments, especially for first-time parents. You may think that you are all prepped to take care of the little one, but things start to get tricky when they won't take food, spend all night crying, and want to be carried in the arms all day long. With parents being so tired and drained all the time, reading to the little one is the last thing on their mind. Reading to them when they are nearly asleep is a great way to start. You can gradually make more time when they are fully awake, well-fed, and in the mood for some play time.

Infants Under One

Infants from birth to three months have blurred vision. It is still developing. Picking books with bigger text or high-contrast pictures is a good way to start. You can also invest in books that are interactive such as the ones that come with puppets, peepholes, or mirrors. The idea is to keep their mind and hands engaged so their gross and motor skills can also improve. Again, though, the idea is to read to them. You can also do so from a magazine. They may not comprehend, but that isn't the point. It is the activity and routine that matter. It is hearing your voice that counts. It is seeing you hold a book or a magazine that makes the difference.

By the time children enter the second half of their first year, they begin to grasp simple words like 'yes,' 'no,' 'mommy,' 'daddy,' etc. These are usually the ones that they hear their parents say the most. At this age, books with a single object per page are a great way to engage them in reading. It can be a book of alphabets, animals, fruits, or numbers. This promotes verbal recognition as well.

When the child repeatedly hears you say a word while looking at a particular object, they begin to form an association. You can also say something and then ask a child to point at what you have said to see if they can make the connection between the word and the object. To further enhance comprehension, you can use your hands, facial expressions, and tone to act out things. For example, if you are saying the word 'lion,' you can put your hands right next to your face, form your palm in the shape of a claw, and roar like a lion.

Babies Under Two

Babies under the age of two are more receptive to your commands and responses. They are at a stage where they can easily identify various objects in a book, if not verbalize them. They are more drawn to your actions than your voice now, so the more you act out, the better. You can read them a story with several characters in different voices. It will be both funny and engaging. For example, you can read to them the story about Goldilocks and the Three Bears and give each bear a different tone of voice. Sooner or later, they will begin to mimic your tone and reply.

Also, if you are reading them a storybook, you can always ask them what will happen next, given that they have heard the story many times. You can also engage in active learning where you ask them to point at stuff in the house. Like, "where's daddy," "where's doggie," "where's the door," etc.

At this age, you can also expand their exposure by showing them pictures of things they don't normally see every day. Most children start to speak by the time they are two, so you will have ample opportunities to ask them questions about a book you read to them. If they answer back, you can boost their vocabulary by repeating the same answer but adding more specifics. For instance, if the toddler can identify a car just by looking at a picture, you can say, "Very good. It's a red car!"

By the time your child turns two, reading will start to reassure and calm them. The routine itself will make them joyous. If they show interest in a particular story or book, don't hesitate to read it to them again and again. Experts believe that it allows children to make sense of what's happening as well as remember the words.

At this stage, you should also read them books about simple experiences like going to the park, walking the dog, taking a bath, etc.

When children request to read one story over and over again, probe them to tell you what's going to happen next. Let them speak and see their level of understanding. This should help you pick your next set of books for them.

Toddlers Under Three

By the time they turn three, they can begin to read and explore books without supervision. They may need some assistance but will do most of the work themselves. They may also show an inclination toward books with more words and longer sentences. You can start to read these to them at bedtime. They should be able to retell you a familiar story. The more details they have memorized, the better.

This is the time when you start to shift their attention from just storybook reading to academic reading where you introduce to them the alphabet song with cues and prompts. You can sing it together. If they are interested in writing with chalk or with a pencil, encourage them to write the first letter of their name or at least recognize what it is and what it sounds like.

Some parents have a difficult time, as the child seems more interested in drawing pictures than writing, but that's all right. Writing is something they can learn and master at school too. If they like to draw pictures, let them draw and color.

At this supple age, your child starts to graduate to real stories where a character tries to fix something or take on a simple quest. The story usually ends on a happy note. Such books mostly have 5–10 sentences in total and about the same number of illustrations. If you are intending to pique interest in nonfiction books, now is the time to begin. At this age, young children pick up new things fast. They love to explore and learn about different worlds, inspiring readers, and various cultures is a great way to keep them engaged.

If books have multiple pictures on a page, followed by some text, ask your child to point out what you are reading about. For example, if the book is about the many sounds animals make and in front of them are three animals (a dog, cat, and cow), inquire whose sound you are making by asking them to point at the picture.

Finally, every time you come across a new word, ask your child if they can guess what it means. If not, try to use it in an example and see if they catch on. If not, provide them with the answer, but in a way that they would remember. For example, if the word is 'drizzling', tell them that the word means light rain, the kind that happened a week ago when their dog enjoyed getting wet in the garden.

Toddlers Four and Five

By the time they turn four, you can begin to focus on feelings and emotions. Children have a hard time understanding their inner stress and worry. Therefore, whenever you come across a situation in a story where the main character feels fear, sadness, or anger, stop and take a moment to explain it to them. Discuss these moments in-depth with them so that they can comprehend them better when they come face to face with them. For example, they know that what they are feeling is anger when another child takes their toy for playing. They know that they feel fear when mommy turns off the light in their room. Discussing these times can help them overcome these emotions and cope with them in healthy ways.

At this stage, children also learn to recognize the signs and labels they see around them. They can tell what the traffic light means. They can identify words that rhyme together. They can easily recall and voice alphabets and identify the letter in their name.

They also graduate from stories with simple plots to multiple-layered stories and secondary plots where more than one event is explained. Despite this complexity, your child should be able to recall these events in the order that they happened. They also know that words are read from left to right and top to bottom.

Children Five and Beyond

By this time, you should have a fully-responsible child in charge of their reading material. Children this age can memorize not just stories but also jokes, rhymes, and poems. They can easily match spoken words with written words when they see them and even spell some basic words correctly. They can write their name correctly, know numbers from 0 to 100, and can come up with imaginative predictions as to what will happen in a story next. If they love to read storybooks, they may even come up with one on their own.

They can read simple books with more than ten sentences. The shorter the sentences, the better. By this age, you don't need to sit and supervise their reading, as they can do it themselves and understand concrete definitions of most of the words in their favorite storybook.

If encouraged, they can also use a word in sentences, recall details, and identify characters in a storybook based on their actions and personality. For example, they can tell apart a grumpy old man from a young and enthusiastic child by the way they walk or talk. They can also arrange story events in a sequence.

Picking Age-Appropriate Books for My Child

As children grow older, they need to move from simple, easy-to-read picture books to ones with multi-layered stories and events. There are hundreds of books that come recommended for a particular age, but since not all children have the same reading ability and may have their unique struggles to work on, how can parents find that perfect fit for them: The kind of book that sits just right with how much they can read, vocabulary set, interest, and engagement, etc.?

Ideally, the right book should be at a child's instructional level. An instructional level determines how much your child can read before they start to become frustrated or distracted. Otherwise the children stop growing as a reader because the activity is no longer fun.

So, the first tip to pick the right book for your child is to choose one that is at their reading level. The goal is the improvement of their literacy and vocabulary skills. However, the book should also pique interest and remain engaging. Books that start with complex plots, too many characters, or a vague and unnecessary description can come off as challenging. They may distract and discourage the young reader from reading. In the same vein, books that are too easy will not give your child any room for further growth either.

Secondly, let your child pick their books. Not only is it a habit you want to nurture in them, but it also leaves children with a sense of independence and accountability. When they are told to pick a book of their choice, they feel like they have been given a Herculean task. They don't just have to pick a book; they have to present a case as to why they think it is the best book for them. That means that they have to critically think of the reasons to justify their choice.

Perform a five-finger vocabulary test. When at a library or bookshop, ask your child to read from a book that you have picked for them. Before reading, ask them to hold up five fingers of one hand. Put down one finger every time they come across a word that is too complex to read or understand. If they only put one or two fingers down, it means that they will be able to read the book with some assistance from you. If they put down all their fingers, it means that the book is too hard for them. This is an easy way to determine their level of reading and comprehension.

A similar test is the comprehension check test, where you ask your child to read a small paragraph and then explain to you what happened. If they can explain the story easily, it means that they fully grasp what's happening. If they have a difficult time explaining the concept, you might want to try another, easier book.

There is another strategy you can use, called the PICK strategy.

PICK is a mnemonic to help young children choose the right book for themselves.

- P represents purpose. Children should ask themselves why they want to read this book.
- I represent their interest. Why does the book interest them?
- C represents comprehension. Can they read the book on their own without assistance?
- K represents knowledge. Children should know if they can use most of the words in the book by themselves in their daily lives or not.

Allowing children to sort through each book in this manner is an excellent way to help them come up with a genuine, intelligence-based decision.

Finally, if you want to be sure about the book you are picking for your child, turn to reviews and rate the book on the internet. Chances are good that there are many people like yourself, eager to help other parents with their book research. Online reviews can give you a better idea of what to expect from the book and at what age you should allow your child to read it.

Chapter 3:

How Reading Changes the Brain?

Reading is an excellent mental stimulation for young children and adults alike. According to one study, reading prevents memory decline and protects against conditions like Alzheimer's and dementia (Wilson et al., 2013). As we grow older, memory decline is a natural process. However, in the experiment, it was noticed that readers experienced that decline at a slower pace than non-readers. The authors of the research also claim that reading helps the brain stay healthy and functional for longer, given that reading becomes a daily activity.

Research at Northcentral University indicated similar conclusions. The lead author, Dr. Wade Fish, reported that participants who read have a slower rate of memory deterioration ("Reading improves memory, concentration, and stress," 2016). They are better at recalling things and remembering intimate details. He also believes that when one enjoys reading about their interests, it builds appreciation toward life and the world. It becomes an out-of-this-world experience and offers readers an escape from the negative cycle of their thoughts.

Scientists at the University of California believe that the act of reading does more than just help heighten overall brain functioning. It also lowers the beta-amyloid levels in the brain, a protein found mostly in Alzheimer's patients (Jagust, 2015). Reading has also been linked to mental flexibility and open-mindedness, creating situations where the reader makes rational decisions based on all sides of the stories (O'Sullivan et al., 2015).

All these studies confirm that brain functioning improves drastically when one develops the habit of reading, but what goes on in the brain when you begin to read? What happens when you give children a book to read or read to them? How does their brain process the information? What sort of pleasure do they experience when they hear their favorite stories? How does the ending make them react?

All these are questions that intrigued several scientists, and it wasn't long before some of them went in and performed an experiment.

What Goes on in the Mind When a Child Reads?

A newly published study by Dr. John Hutton offers some valuable insights as to what happens inside the brain of young ones when they read or are read to. He calls it the Goldilocks effect. He believes that there are different kinds of storytelling—some too hot, too cold, and some just right. Hutton is an avid reader himself and obsessed with the concept of emergent literacy: the process of learning to read.

In the study, he gathered twenty-seven four-year-olds and had their brains scanned by an fMRI machine. While their brains were being scanned, the children presented stories in three different formats. The first was audio-only, the second illustrated pages with an audio voiceover, and the third an animated cartoon. As the little ones heard those stories, the machine captured any form of activation within the brain networks and their connectivity. They already had an idea of what brain networks would be influenced by the story. One was language, the second was visual perception, and third was visual imagery. To their surprise, though, there was another default mode network he calls the seat of the soul. It was internal reflection. Children, while hearing those stories, tried to connect with the story and question how it mattered to them.

The default mode network included regions of the brain which are generally active when we aren't actively focusing on a designated mental task. Here's what he found:

In the first story format where the children only heard the audio, the condition was too cold. Although language networks were activated, there was little to no connectivity overall. In short, the children seem to have a difficult time trying to understand.

In the third format, animation format, there was a lot of activity between the visual and auditory perception networks but little connectivity among the other brain networks. The animation was doing most of the work for the children. They seemed to be expending all their energy on trying to figure out what it means. In this format, their comprehension of the story was the worst.

In the illustration plus voiceover formation, it felt just right. When children could see the illustrations, their language-network activity slowed down a bit. They were no longer paying attention to just the words. Their understanding and comprehension of the story were aided by the illustrations that followed.

With animation, it felt like the entire story was dumped on them and they had little time to do the math. With animation plus audio, the brain's most important regions showed the greatest connectivity and activation.

This suggests that when we read to our children from an illustrated book, we allow them to develop their brain muscles and bring those images to life in their heads.

Chapter 4:

The Positive Impacts of Reading on the Mind

It doesn't matter if you read fiction or nonfiction with your child—reading improves their knowledge about the world and themselves. This knowledge can come to them in the form of a poem, a news article from a magazine, or an educational coursebook. Reading is both informative and entertaining. Throughout the years, researchers, scientists, and doctors have confirmed that reading reduces stress and lowers blood pressure and heart rate. These medical reasons aside, though, the reason we experience a true pleasure from reading is that it allows us to live our dreams and fantasies. The same happens for children too.

When they read about an astronaut that saved the world from a gigantic asteroid, they believe anything is possible. When they read survival stories, they believe that they can overcome any struggle in their lives too. When they listen to stories about family bonding or pursuing a passion, they believe that they can be an excellent, important, and valuable part of their community. This is how they learn to develop empathy and compassion. Readers learn to be in other people's shoes and relate to their stories. Reading changes their perception about viewing others and themselves. When they read a story about an underprivileged character, they become more grateful for the things and people they have. This boosts their appreciation for life, and in that process takes away some of the stress they feel.

Those are a lot of bold claims, though. How can a simple act of reading do all that? Luckily, there is some explanation. Most great ideas take birth in the mind; so does the art of reading. You may have never noticed this, but when you see a word on a page, your brain starts to create a mental image of it in the mind. Think about an apple and, in less than a second, you have a mental image of it. You can also be as specific as you want, and it still will work the same. For example, think of a green apple with a worm coming out of it. You have that image in your head right now too. The point is, despite being super busy, our brain has the superpower to analyze words or auditory detection and visualize. This is what happens when we read. When we read a story, a description isn't always needed. Our brain has the power to create a strong mental image of itself.

Now that you know, it seems more magical than it did before. Below are some ways reading affects your brain and what it can mean for your child's development:

Reading also amplifies brain connectivity. You might have met or heard someone say that a particular book changed their life. It's uncommon, but some devoted fans would gulp down everything that their favorite author wrote. To them, their words become like medicine. They feel empowered and in control when they read their books. Now imagine the same power but with greater force. Any good book can do that for your child. Researchers believe that reading a narrative prompts changes in the brain. It triggers activity in an otherwise resting brain.

When children read, they don't just take in the words; their little brain tries to paint a vivid picture of the scene, their favorite character, and the plot. The reason they can predict the future is because brain connectivity to and forth the language and perception region improves. In simpler words, the connection between the left frontal cortices, a region associated with language reception, is heightened. Another amazing fact: This activity doesn't end when the child puts down the book. It continues for days following that read (Berns et al., 2013).

Figuratively speaking, it puts the readers in the character's shoes. Research conducted by Emory University experts suggests that reading a novel or story increases activity not just in the frontal temporal cortex but also in the central sulcus of the brain. This region is responsible for the basic sensory-motor activity. When we read a book, neurons in this region activate a special sensation that allows us to experience what the author is describing. For instance, if you are reading the story about the boy who cried wolf, your young one can imagine and experience all that the central character feels. If they are reading Harry Potter and come across the part where Harry tries to run away from

Dementors, the neurons in the central sulcus activate the sensations one experiences when they are physically trying to run.

Reading also enhances your child's working memory. Scientists refer to reading as a neurobiologically challenging activity. They call it a one-of-a-kind activity where the brain does so much more than one would expect. Reading allows readers to improve memory by absorbing more information. This also increases the brain's capacity to store memories. Researchers at the Haskins Laboratories for the Science of the Spoken and Written Word believe that reading, unlike listening to a song or watching a movie, gives the brain more time to stop and follow-through (Berninger et al., 2006). Readers can process what's going on by taking in the information at their own pace. This increases mental activity and helps the memory remain sharp.

If you want to look at it in simpler terms, it looks a lot like lifting weights to build muscles. The more you work out, the more flexible and hardcore your muscles become. Reading and processing what's written at the same time boosts mental activity in the same way.

Reading changes a brain's structure in a good way. Did you know even poor readers who don't appreciate good literature, or read for pleasure can be trained to become better readers? Researchers believe that training the brain via reading can change it (Keller & Just, 2009). Reading increases the white matter in the brain. White matter allows us to be more imaginative, think outside of the box, and be creative. Reading can do that for the brain and improve our productivity, improve our thought processes, and cut back on negative feedback we receive from our inner critics all the time.

Chapter 5:

Where Does Technology Come In?

For many millennia, reading was considered a rich people's activity. It was limited to a few. Only some people had the privilege to buy and stock books. Workers had little time to read because they were out in the fields or factories working full-day jobs. They didn't have the luxury of even a few spare hours in the day to enjoy a pleasurable read. Books, during that era, were also expensive to print and publish. There were few buyers and therefore, the art wasn't as lucrative as expected. Most books were written by hand, so there was always the case of spilled ink and misplacement of papers. Apart from all that, not many people were literate enough to read, let alone read a book.

During the 15th century, some changes appeared when Johannes Guttenberg invented the first printing press. Literacy rates started to rise. The Industrial Revolution expedited the process of mass paper production. Reading newspapers, novels, and newsletters became mainstream, giving rise to many local libraries and bookshops.

Today, the change is even more rapid and transformational. We have graduated from hardcopy books to screens that promise a more vibrant, adjustable, and prominent text structure. With the advent of the internet, readers can read books in various formats on E-readers, phones, and tablets.

This has changed the way we consume words and new knowledge. We have quicker means of accessing specific information in seconds. Many people believe that this is a positive change, but not everyone agrees, as there are some cons to it too.

"What is best for my screen, a screen or a book?" has become a commonly asked question by parents on various online and offline platforms. They are worried about too much exposure via screens but also worry that if they hold back, their child might give up reading.

Let's look at the pros and cons of each and decide.

How Technology Is Changing the Way We Read

Neuroscientists believe that scanning shorter texts, like we do on the internet, changes the way we process information. It changes the wiring inside the brain, making it sharper and quicker at searching for a specific keyword, piece of information, or solution. Our research skills improve, and so do our scanning skills. At the same time, though, it also renders us unable to read longer texts with focus, a given with printed books.

Another perk of reading books on screens is unlimited resources. If you want your child to read a specific book, you don't have to go down to the library and physically look for it in the archives. You can just type in a search engine and read it online within minutes of the start of your quest. This makes reading on-screen a time-saving activity. Your child can spend that extra time examining and critically analyzing the information.

Via the internet, you can also reserve a book online and then go to your nearest library to pick it up in person. At the same time, going to the library and searching for a specific book in the aisles is another kind of adventure you don't want your child to miss out on. The act of searching increases their chances to come across books that they would like to read after they are done reading the one they came looking for.

Online reading has paved the way for some amazing e-book reading services like Oyster, Scribd, and Entitle. Each platform houses more than 100,000 books, giving its subscribers a vast range of educational media to choose from.

With e-books, your child no longer has to physically carry a book everywhere they go. If they like to hear a story on the way to their grandma's, they can do so with the help of an audiobook. Imagine the chaos when they realize they have forgotten their favorite book at home when you have covered half the distance. You know the fussing and crying won't end until you go back and get it.

E-books and audiobooks are more interactive in nature. There are many add-ons like improved text visibility, bigger text, various fonts and colors, zoom in and out, etc. that young ones may enjoy using. They can also click on words they find difficult to read and listen to their correct pronunciation in a second. The same applies to words they find hard to understand.

On-screen reading caters to a child's special needs and unique reading/learning styles. When children are made to read from a book or have someone read to them, there is little anonymity. Their struggles are out there for the world to make fun of, especially in the classrooms. Devices make struggling readers feel less embarrassed about their reading/learning levels. They can instantly look up words that they pronounced wrong and look for meanings of the ones they didn't understand. The ease of recommendations also empowers them to read a book that fits their skills and interest level.

Of course, it's not all good, is it? There have to be some unique advantages that only a print format can offer.

For starters, print books offer two components: the physical medium and the mindset we bring to reading on that particular medium. Everything else just follows from there. Since the primary use of screens is for social connections and amusement, both adults and children can have a difficult time remaining focused on them. There is also little time for them to absorb new information since it was designed to be read casually and quickly. So, when it comes to reading something that demands our focus and attention, we fail. We fail to fully grasp the core ideas.

For early readers, print books are by far the best option there is. It makes it easier for children and parents to interact with language. With a print medium, parents can have a question and answer session too, called dialogic reading, which isn't possible with screen books.

This was revealed during a 2019 study where researchers found that there was little spoken activity between the parent and the child when they read through a screen medium (Munzer et al., 2019). They were more engaged at looking at the device than at the text. In short, there was less social back-and-forth involved. This suggests that there was limited bonding and connection between the parent and the child.

Apart from that, many salient features that come with a screen can be distracting. The images, although added to make the story more interesting, can take away the attention from the core message of the book, leaving young readers wondering what to make of it. On the other hand, with print books, there can be a healthy discussion about the moral of the story with the parent, promising rich dialogue exchange and time well-spent. This also proves to be valuable as it integrates knowledge learned from the story with life experience. Reading from a print version of a story allows children to think, slow down, and process things deeply.

Additionally, if children are only exposed to devices and not physical books, they lose the tactile experience of handling one. By reading a book, they learn to scroll through the pages, read from left to right and top to bottom. They can also share books with their friends. Technology can't replace that.

Finally, with real books, children can cuddle with their parents or gather around a teacher to listen to what they read. Storytime is an engaging activity, and it only remains one when two play at it at the same time. When children read from a physical book, they associate reading with nurturing. With devices, parents become more cautious of what the child is doing on the device rather than focusing on the real story and the core values it represents.

A Balancing Act

So, which is it? Are eBooks better, or should we stick to the good ol' print versions of our favorite stories? Honestly speaking, strike a balance. On days when reading to your child seems impossible because you had a tough day at work, stick with a tablet or MacBook. On other days where you have the free time to spend with the kids and engage in some healthy activity, take up a book from the shelf and start to read. The goal isn't to compare; the goal is to develop a healthy habit of reading regardless of the medium they choose.

Additionally, look at what your child is more comfortable with. Younger children are more drawn to the physicality of things. An interactive book with pictures popping out, with buttons to push, and with music to play is a great activity. It can be difficult to make them sit and look at a screen. There is always the risk of them trying to grab it by their hands and put their teeth on it. If they are old enough to maneuver the swipes and turn from one page to another without assistance, you can call the transition a positive one. Besides, having to choose a book that piques their interest also becomes easier in this case as many apps and websites show recommended reads based on your child's taste alongside. They can always click on them and try to read. They can skip and move on to the next one if they find it boring or difficult.

Finally, don't stress if your child ditches reading from a physical book entirely. Trying to force them into it by limiting screen time can come off as a negative experience. The child might lose all the garnered interest they had in reading. Even if they continue to read from a book, they may not be as engaged as before. Therefore, don't make it something like a point you have to prove that hardcopy books are better than on-screen media.

You want to raise a willing reader that enjoys what they do, not someone that is forced to do so.

Chapter 6:

Struggling Readers

Reading disorders or difficulties occur when children have trouble reading basic words or comprehending basic sentences. Most reading difficulties result from how the brain processes written words and text. Not many parents are aware, but these difficulties could be genetic and passed on to your children. Some children can also develop reading and comprehension problems from an injury to the brain during infancy.

It isn't hard to spot children having difficulty with reading and comprehension. Sometimes, they forget commonly used words, pronounce words wrong, or make the mistake of writing mirrored texts like writing a "b" instead of a "d." Some children may be poor spellers, too.

Some of the most common reading difficulties that children face include decoding, comprehension, phonemic issues, and retention problems. Let's look at each of these individually and notice any signs that you should be worried about.

Decoding Issues

Children with decoding issues face problems with breaking down the phonemes in order to spell out a sentence correctly. For example, a child without a decoding inability may easily separate the different sounds in the word "table" or "chalk" without assistance. A child with a decoding disability may not. They might not judge the meaning between the simple letters, what sound they make when combined together, and how to voice them.

Signs to watch out for include issues in sounding words, lack of expression in reading, difficulty in recognizing separate words, missing punctuation marks when reading, slow speed, and confusion between letters and their sounds.

Phonemic Awareness Issues

A child may be unable to read words from a page for a lot of reasons. They may have a sensory processing disorder where they can't visually see the text. They may have trouble making a connection between the written word and their sounds or have any of these conditions:

- Dyslexia: Inability to decode word sounds
- Autism Spectrum Disorder: A development disorder that affects how the brain understands sound speech

- Irlen Syndrome: A disruption in the brain's ability to process visual information.

Comprehension Issues

Comprehension of any written or spoken material is only possible when the child successfully decodes it. However, when the child fails to do so, they can have a difficult time understanding what they are reading or remembering it afterward. Repetition, in this case, can be very exhausting, especially when the child is reading coursebooks. Signs that your child may have comprehension difficulty include confusing words and their meanings, inability to use words in sentences, difficulty in connecting ideas in different paragraphs, difficulty distinguishing important information from minor details, glossing over details, omitting details, and lack of focus during reading, etc.

Signs My Child Has Reading Problems

Although the signs mentioned before do paint a picture of what to look for, many of them go unnoticed and neglected. Parents simply label it as mischief and lack of discipline on the child's part, blaming them for putting in a weak effort. Since the core of the issue remains unaddressed and the child barely understands what's wrong with them, reading and comprehension problems often go undetected for long periods. They only come to light when the child consistently performs poorly on a test and comes home with bad grades. That is when the parents start to question what could be wrong.

However, by the time they do, the child has already lost most of their confidence and willingness to read. There is little to no excitement, as the past poor experiences are enough to remind them of how bad they perceive themselves to be.

If one pays attention, though, these signs can be spotted earlier and offer parents and teachers a chance to work with the child in a unique and more focused manner. It is also important to note that reading or comprehension issues aren't developmental issues. They don't suggest lower intelligence among children.

Below are some more detectable signs to look for when in your child, as they might have an unaddressed reading issue:

A child that shows no interest in reading, no matter how amazing and engaging the books are. If a child deliberately avoids reading and throws a tantrum whenever they are told to write something or read out a paragraph aloud indicates poor comprehension and reading issues. This isn't a chronic condition, as most of the fear of reading stems from a lack of confidence in their abilities. Since the child keeps making mistakes, they feel frustrated to a point where they want to avoid reading altogether.

Another possible reason can be difficulty in following basic instructions or directions. This isn't a pressing issue because this doesn't indicate that the child has trouble with reading or spelling words out. It is a sign that they have trouble comprehending the ideas suggested or following them as they are. To further test if this is the case, instruct your child to do something. Then, instruct them again, but this time, add two or more instructions in the same sentence. Chances are good that your child will be confused and only follow the first or second direction accurately.

Difficulty in pronouncing or recognizing words is another sign that your child suffers from a reading disorder. When a child fails to repeatedly pronounce or recognize a word correctly, they become so focused on the problem that they forget about the context of the text. When this happens, there is no memory of what was read earlier or what the text was about, which affects their self-esteem and leaves children ready to give up on reading.

Reading comprehension is an art where you understand what you are reading. It might sound simple, but some kids have a challenging time doing so. They can't picture what they are reading. They can't create an image of a setting, person, or object like we can when we hear a specific word. They need more time to process and understand what they are reading and then create a mental image.

If your child requires too long to perform basic tasks, they may have a problem with reading comprehension. This happens mostly when instructions are provided in the written format. Think of it as an adult having a hard time reading and following through on the instructions on how to assemble an IKEA table. If your child demonstrates similar struggles with a basic task, they may have comprehension issues.

Chapter 7:

Reluctant Readers: When Reading Becomes a Forced Activity

Some young readers don't have any difficulty with reading or comprehension. They just don't want to read. Despite having the means to afford a book or read from a device, they choose not to. We call them reluctant readers. This happens when a child shows little interest in the activity of reading. There can be several reasons for that.

For starters, difficulties can be due to the fact that the child lacks effective role models to look up to. Households, where parents aren't readers themselves, have a difficult time raising readers. It is because most of the learning that happens during the initial years of their development happens via interaction and sight. They imitate actions, behaviors, and habits. Non-reader parents don't give their children the exposure they need to view reading as a pleasurable activity. When they fail to experience the pleasures that can come from reading a story, they miss out on a lot of great times.

Besides, reading a book isn't only for your wellness, it does wonders for your brain, attention, focus, and emotions, as covered in the former chapter. From building vocabulary to identifying sounds and from gaining more knowledge about the unknown to exploring new adventures with their favorite characters, there is so much that a good book offers.

In this final chapter, we deal with the question, "How to get children excited about reading?" another pressing concern with parents of young ones. Before we talk about how to intrigue engagement, let's review some common reasons why reluctant readers are born.

Why Isn't My Child Excited About Reading?

There is no easy way to say this, but some children just don't like to read. They don't get the same joy others get when they read a story, go on quests with the main character, and cry and roll down in a ball when someone dies. We all want our children to become avid readers, and we try to give them the best, yet they just don't catch the same excitement. Here are some possible reasons for that:

Reading difficulty is the #1 reason why children don't like to read. When they secretly know that they lack the knowledge or expertise to do so, they don't want to do it. Every time someone brings up reading, they feel like they are going to fail at it all over again. This feeling isn't pleasant. If anything, it takes away their confidence.

A lack of routine and structure can also be one of the contributing factors. Some days parents are available to read and spend time with the child and other days, there is no mention of reading. Even if the child wants to read, lack of time on their hands prevents it. This stops reading from becoming an everyday ritual, and thus, the habit never solidifies.

Some children never get the chance to have access to quality books that would otherwise engage one to read and explore further. In some households, only course books are considered worthy of a read, and we can all attest that no kid likes their math book enough to read from it every day. Children who never experience what happiness reading can bring due to lack of access also become reluctant readers.

Reading books that don't interest young children also makes them reluctant readers. Some books and genres just aren't the right fit. For example, you might press your child to read novels while they are more into graphic comic books. In other cases, some books seem so out of their depth that they fail to comprehend what's being said. This causes stress and frustration, both of which can make them reluctant readers.

Reading may also stop appealing to young children when they are presented with other more visually stimulating experiences like video games and watching videos on YouTube. They lose interest because in video games and cartoon videos, the story is being told to you without any effort on your part. That seems more rewarding.

Maybe it is the wrong format for them. They may not be into print media. They may enjoy reading more on a tablet or phone.

How to Get My Child into Reading

A child may begin to read with passion and conviction, provided they are given the right tools and resources to work with. For example, infants and toddlers do well with books that they can hold in their hands, have chunky cardboard pages they won't tear through, and are intentionally interactive to improve attention. They may also enjoy books with lots of colorful but simple illustrations to improve memory recall. Through these images, they can learn to associate the objects with their names and sounds.

If you hand them a book too big for them to hold, chances are good that they will be too distracted by the gigantic size of it to immerse in the story. Similarly, if the book is just text, they will have little to focus on. If the illustrations are too complex for them to make sense of, they will avoid reading. If all these conditions persist, there will be little to no reading.

So, how do you get them to read? Let's see.

Sing to an infant to hold their attention. Simple books with lullabies or sounds of animals are great in this context. As a parent, you can voice out different characters to keep the little one excited.

You can also play peek-a-boo with flap books if they are too young to be read to.

Give them books to touch and feel. There are different textures that books for young children come in. Having the feel of the many textures will also excite them about the book and the story.

For older children, encourage having conversations and discussions about the storyline, character personalities, and feelings they experience. Ask for their opinion about a particular action and see how they respond. This will give you a better idea of what to pick next for them. When they share their ideas and thoughts about the story, listen without judgment or criticism. This will show them that their feelings are valued and validated. When they feel understood and appreciated, they will be more likely to engage in another book.

Let them read to you. As soon as they start to read basic sentences, encourage them to read aloud to you. You can always start if the child seems shy. As they read, don't be too quick to point out a mistake or pronunciation error. Doing so will discourage them. Wait until they are done reading a page before you correct them.

Set up a designated reading spot in the house for your child. Make sure that it is a distraction-free spot. Let the child read peacefully when they are in the zone. Decorate the zone with a shelf where the child can stack their favorite collection, providing some snacks so that the child can eat and some stationary in case the child wants to highlight or underline some words. You can also 'DIY' some bookmarks for their books. They are simple to craft and you two can color and decorate them as you like.

Look for book-inspired activities. For example, if your child loves reading books about the Air Force, you can take them to an Air Force museum. If they love to read about the animals, the zoo is an ideal place to go over the weekend. If they love to read about the stars, how about a trip to the planetarium? There is always some activity or place you can be to get kids more excited about the possibilities there are. You can also plan yearly vacations to places that your child has read about in a book. For instance, if they are fascinated by the backstory of the Statue of Liberty, you can all go on a trip to view it up close.

There are also many great books that were made into movies: classics like *The Lord of the Rings trilogy, Harry Potter, Peter Pan, Cat in the Hat, Charlie and the Chocolate Factory*, etc. Having read the books, the children already have a mental image of what the characters and setting would look like. Watching it being portrayed on the big screen is another type of euphoria. Surely, your young one will be delighted to watch their favorite characters come alive from the pages of the book and onto the screens. You can even host a movie night once the child has finished reading the book and celebrate it as a family together.

Make library trips extra special. Plan it beforehand to get the excitement flowing. Once you are there, ask them to pick at least three books of their choosing. Let them spend some time going through the many available options. Help them refine their search skills by telling them how to sort through themes and alphabets. Once they are done picking their favorites, take them up to the librarian and hand them the money. Once out, make a whole day out of it by going for a quick snack someplace and then head home to begin reading from their new collection.

Oh, and don't forget to get them a library card. Most public libraries issue cards when a child turns five with their name on them. For avid readers, this is no less than a medal. Let them keep it in a safe place where they can feel joy looking at it. While at the library, check out library reading hours and any special programs or book reading sessions they have for the kids on weekends.

For events like Halloween, have them go as their favorite character from a book. Dressing as their favorite character will make them feel like a superhero with all the powers and skills that the character boasts. It can be a fun way to get children on board with the idea that books are more than just for reading. You can even role-play some of their favorite scenes from the book.

Conclusion

Reading from an early age to infants and toddlers does have some promising benefits. As discussed in the book on various occasions, we are left with no choice but to ensure that we are raising an avid reader at home. From changing the way their brain functions to how it reduces stress and improves wellbeing, reading has remained a pleasurable activity for centuries. It boosts intelligence, makes one compassionate, enhances creativity and imagination, and allows us to be so many things at the same time.

Books are portals to different worlds and cultures. They are the best way to time travel and get lost in rich traditions, festivities, and realms. With so many genres to choose from, it is hard to say that one won't find a book of their liking.

Thanks to technology that plays its part too, we are now living in an era where reading a book is always an option. All we need are readers who are as passionate as the people who write those books.

So, let's pledge to raise children who love to read. Who is excited by the thought of getting a new book at Christmas as opposed to getting a new PS5? Let's raise a generation that will willingly take the time for a self-care activity like reading and step into a different world.

Let's build healthy reading habits so that our children have an easy time with their grades and academics. Let them experience the joy of reading, and, hopefully, we will have a generation that cares about others, is empathic, curious, creative, and—above all—intelligent.

Thank you for giving this book a read. I hope you loved reading it as much as I enjoyed writing it. It would make me the happiest person on earth if you would take a moment to leave an honest review. All you have to do is visit the site where you purchased this book: It's that simple! The review doesn't have to be a full-fledged paragraph; a few words will do. Your few words will help others decide if this is what they should be reading as well. Thank you in advance, and best of luck with your parenting adventures. Every moment is a joyous one with a child.

References

Allen, L., & Kelly, B. B. (2015, July 23). *Child development and early learning*. Nih.gov; National Academies Press (US). https://www.ncbi.nlm.nih.gov/books/NBK310550/

Are readers more successful? (2021, November 3). SuperSummary. https://www.supersummary.com/are-readers-more-successful/

Babbin, E. (n.d.). *6 reasons why kids refuse to read.* Www.understood.org. https://www.understood.org/articles/en/6-reasons-why-kids-refuse-to-read

Balmain, M. (2002, September 8). *Age-by-Age guide to reading to your baby*. Parents. https://www.parents.com/baby/development/

intellectual/age-by-age-guide-to-reading-to-your-baby/

Ben-Aharon, A. (2019, April 19). *Signs of reading problems in children & adults*. Great Speech. https://greatspeech.com/7-signs-of-reading-comprehension-problems-in-children-and-adults/

Berninger, V. W., Abbott, R. D., Vermeulen, K., & Fulton, C. M. (2006). Paths to reading comprehension in at-risk second-grade readers. *Journal of Learning Disabilities*, *39*(4), 334–351. https://doi.org/10.1177/00222194060390040701

Berns, G. S., Blaine, K., Prietula, M. J., & Pye, B. E. (2013). Short- and long-term effects of a novel on connectivity in the brain. *Brain Connectivity*, *3*(6), 590–600. https://doi.org/10.1089/brain.2013.0166

Carnegie mellon scientists discover first evidence of brain rewiring in children - carnegie mellon university | CMU. (2020). Cmu.edu.

https://www.cmu.edu/news/archive/2009/December/dec9_brainrewiringevidence.shtml

Castro, D. (2015, February 27). *Benefits of reading to your child.* CCE Suffolk County Family Health & Wellness. https://blogs.cornell.edu/ccesuffolkfhw/2015/02/27/benefits-of-reading-to-your-child/

Choosing age-appropriate books for your child. (2016, August 4). Educational Playcare. https://www.educationalplaycare.com/blog/choosing-appropriate-books-for-your-child/

Chow, D. (n.d.). *5 possible reasons why your child dislikes reading.* The New Age Parents. Retrieved November 5, 2021, from https://thenewageparents.com/5-possible-reasons-why-your-child-dislikes-reading/

Cleveland, T. (2017, March 23). *Eight tips to get kids excited about reading.* Reading Partners. https://readingpartners.org/blog/eight-tips-get-kids-excited-reading/

Collier, E. (2019, May 24). *Why is reading so important for children?* The Hub | High Speed Training; High Speed Training. https://www.highspeedtraining.co.uk/hub/why-is-reading-important-for-children/

Deam, J. (2019). *E-Books vs. print: What parents need to know*. Scholastic. https://www.scholastic.com/parents/books-and-reading/reading-resources/developing-reading-skills/e-books-vs-print-what-parents-need-to-know.html

Duursma, E., Augustyn, M., & Zuckerman, B. (2008). Reading aloud to children: The evidence. *Archives of Disease in Childhood*, *93*(7), 554–557. https://doi.org/10.1136/adc.2006.106336

High, P. (2014, June 24). I is for infant: Reading aloud to young children benefits brain development (J. Brown, Interviewer) [Interview]. In *PBS NewsHour*. https://www.pbs.org/newshour/show/infant-reading-aloud-young-children-benefits-brain-development

How technology is changing our reading habits. (n.d.). Readers Digest. https://www.readersdigest.co.uk/lifestyle/technology/how-technology-is-changing-our-reading-habits

How technology is changing our reading habits. (2017, August 28). DailySabah. https://www.dailysabah.com/feature/2017/08/29/how-technology-is-changing-our-reading-habits

Hutton, J. S., Huang, G., Sahay, R. D., DeWitt, T., & Ittenbach, R. F. (2020). A novel, composite measure of screen-based media use in young children (screenq) and associations with parenting practices and cognitive abilities. *Pediatric Research*. https://doi.org/10.1038/s41390-020-0765-1

Importance of reading to your children | children's bureau. (2017, March 3). Child Abuse Prevention,

Treatment & Welfare Services | Children's Bureau. https://www.all4kids.org/news/blog/the-importance-of-reading-to-your-children/

Jagust, W. (2015). Is amyloid-β harmful to the brain? Insights from human imaging studies. *Brain*, *139*(1), 23–30. https://doi.org/10.1093/brain/awv326

Kamenetz, A. (2018, May 24). *What's going on in your child's brain when you read them A story?* NPR.org. https://www.npr.org/sections/ed/2018/05/24/611609366/whats-going-on-in-your-childs-brain-when-you-read-them-a-story

Keller, T. A., & Just, M. A. (2009). Altering cortical connectivity: Remediation-Induced changes in the white matter of poor readers. *Neuron*, *64*(5), 624–631. https://doi.org/10.1016/j.neuron.2009.10.018

King, J. (2013, July 28). *Readers vs non-readers*. Reading. Writing. Spying.

https://spywriter.wordpress.com/2013/07/28/readers-vs-non-readers/

Klass, P. (2021, March 16). How children read differently from books vs. screens. *New York Times.* https://www.nytimes.com/2021/03/16/well/family/children-reading-screens-books.html

Marcin, A. (2020, October 14). *Reading to children: Why it's so important and how to start.* Healthline. https://www.healthline.com/health/childrens-health/reading-to-children#benefits

McNamee, D. (2014, July 26). *Childhood reading skills linked to "higher intelligence" in young adults.* Www.medicalnewstoday.com. https://www.medicalnewstoday.com/articles/280193

Miller, E. C. (2017, June 17). *7 ways readers think differently than non-readers.* Bustle. https://www.bustle.com/p/7-ways-readers-think-differently-than-non-readers-63688

Milne, V. (2020, May 4). *An age-by-age guide to reading to your kids*. Today's Parent. https://www.todaysparent.com/family/parenting/reading-to-kids-age-by-age-guide/#gallery/books-for-4-and-5-year-olds/slide-2

Misunderstood minds . reading difficulties | PBS. (2019). Pbs.org. https://www.pbs.org/wgbh/misunderstoodminds/readingdiffs.html

Munzer, T. G., Miller, A. L., Weeks, H. M., Kaciroti, N., & Radesky, J. (2019). Differences in parent-toddler interactions with electronic versus print books. *Pediatrics*, *143*(4). https://doi.org/10.1542/peds.2018-2012

O'Sullivan, N., Davis, P., Billington, J., Gonzalez-Diaz, V., & Corcoran, R. (2015). "Shall I compare thee": The neural basis of literary awareness, and its benefits to cognition. *Cortex*, *73*, 144–157. https://doi.org/10.1016/j.cortex.2015.08.014

Parrish, N. (2020, February 3). *5 ways to support students who struggle with reading comprehension*. Edutopia. https://www.edutopia.org/article/5-ways-support-students-who-struggle-reading-comprehension

Phillips, N. (2012, September 7). *This is your brain on jane austen, and stanford researchers are taking notes*. Stanford University. https://news.stanford.edu/news/2012/september/austen-reading-fmri-090712.html#:~:text=The%20researchers%20found%20that%20blood

Reading and storytelling with babies and children. (2018, June 22). Raising Children Network. https://raisingchildren.net.au/babies/play-learning/literacy-reading-stories/reading-storytelling

Reading improves memory, concentration and stress. (2016, December 10). Northcentral University. https://www.ncu.edu/blog/reading-improves-memory-concentration-and-stress#gref

Reading milestones. (2018, June). Kidshealth.org. https://kidshealth.org/en/parents/milestones.html

Reading problems: Types, best strategies & solutions for struggling readers. (2019, April 22). Www.kidsacademy.mobi. https://www.kidsacademy.mobi/storytime/reading-problems/

Ritchie, S. J., Bates, T. C., & Plomin, R. (2014). Does learning to read improve intelligence? A longitudinal multivariate analysis in identical twins from age 7 to 16. *Child Development*, *86*(1), 23–36. https://doi.org/10.1111/cdev.12272

Ruddy, E. Z. (2017, January 17). *18 genius ways to make kids love reading.* Parents. https://www.parents.com/toddlers-preschoolers/development/reading/18-genius-ways-to-make-kids-love-reading/

Smith, S. R. (n.d.). *Common reading problems in children.* See-N-Read. Retrieved November 5, 2021, from http://www.see-n-read.com/common-reading-problems-in-children/

Stephanie. (n.d.). Tips for choosing age appropriate kid books. *Parenting Chaos.* https://parentingchaos.com/choosing-age-appropriate-kid-books/

Trombetta, S. (2017a, May 15). *Why reading is the best workout for your brain.* Bustle; Bustle. https://www.bustle.com/p/why-reading-is-the-best-workout-for-your-brain-57441

Trombetta, S. (2017b, August 11). *5 astonishing ways reading changes your brain.* Bustle. https://www.bustle.com/p/what-does-reading-do-to-your-brain-these-5-effects-are-pretty-astounding-74676

Ward, J. (2020, December 12). *How is technology changing the way we read?* Medium. https://medium.com/technology-hits/how-is-technology-changing-the-way-we-read-7ddce817b797

Wilson, R. S., Boyle, P. A., Yu, L., Barnes, L. L., Schneider, J. A., & Bennett, D. A. (2013). Life-span cognitive activity, neuropathologic burden, and cognitive aging. *Neurology, 81*(4), 314–321. https://doi.org/10.1212/wnl.0b013e31829c5e8a

Wolf, M. C., Muijselaar, M. M. L., Boonstra, A. M., & de Bree, E. H. (2018). The relationship between reading and listening comprehension: Shared and modality-specific components. *Reading and Writing, 32*(7), 1747–1767. https://doi.org/10.1007/s11145-018-9924-8

Your brain on books: 10 ways reading affects psyche. (2016, March 31). OEDB.org. https://oedb.org/ilibrarian/your-brain-on-books-10-things-that-happen-to-our-minds-when-we-read/

www.ingramcontent.com/pod-product-compliance
Lightning Source LLC
LaVergne TN
LVHW051018080826
845145LV00009B/2693

* 9 7 8 1 9 5 6 0 1 8 2 4 0 *